CW00871998

FREEDOM IN T

*How we escaped and built a
bungalow and pool resort*

By Dave James

Copyright © 2021 Dave James

All Rights Reserved

CONTENTS

INTRODUCTION

This book is about finding freedom in an unfree world and our story of how we escaped the restrictive UK and built a beautiful bungalow and swimming pool resort in Issan, Northeast Thailand. The sad thing is that most people in the western world actually believe they are free, but in reality, are trapped in the system and live week to week or month to month, with no ability to save money due to the horrendous rents, council tax and all the other bills and regulations one is caught up in.

After travelling the world several times in my lifetime, Thailand is probably one of the best and most freedom loving places I have ever lived and have now retired to. It's not for everyone as many people get culture shock when they come here for the first time and can't stand how the Thais think and get things done. And even after over 30 years of living in and out of Thailand, even I am still shocked at the things we see every time we venture out of our little paradise resort into clown-world. Like the many motorbikes driving the wrong way towards us on the inside lane, everyone wearing masks but no crash helmets and the crazy accidents they show on Thai TV every night, has to be seen to be believed. This is truly like living in the Twilight zone.

But Thailand also has is good side, fantastic scenery, nature, beaches, amazing food, the weather can be extreme but is still beautiful, five star hospitals, no waiting lists to see a doctor for anything as one can go private for very little money. Amazing shopping centres in Bangkok and Phuket but the most important thing,

 is how FREE I feel compared to living in the UK.

CHAPTER 1

What is Freedom?

L et's take a look at freedom or being a FREE MAN. Have you ever heard of the "Freeman" concept or way of life? Look it up for an in depth interpretation of what it means and how the "elites" have created a banking and legal system that keeps virtually everyone busy, in debt, occupied and enslaved.

Why do you think they named the job you do, your OCCUPA-TION.

Why do you think they are called T V PROGRAMS.

What about the word Government, Govern means control and ment is the mind. (Mind Control)

The Matrix movie was probably one of the best analogies of how 95% of everyone you know and meet on a daily basis are living their lives, totally asleep and stuck in the matrix. In fact many claim it is not a movie but a documentary of which I fully agree. But like Neo in the movie, you don't know you're asleep until you take the red pill and see what's really going on, then there's no going back.

A another good movie by Spielberg was, *Joe Versus the Volcano* and critics said it was his poor attempt at comedy, but they totally missed the underlying meaning of the movie. It stars Meg Ryan,

Lloyd Bridges and Tom Hanks as guy that has a dead end office job, no future, just a boring mundane existence. He ends up at a doctors office and is diagnosed with "brain fog" a terminal illness. Unbeknown to him, the doctor lied as he worked for a very rich guy (I think was the owner of the company he worked for played by Lloyd Bridges) and owned a volcanic island in the South Pacific. And Tom Hanks accepts an offer to briefly "live like a king, die like a man", but to fulfil his agreement, he must willingly jump into the live volcano on the island of Waponi Woo in order to appease the volcano god.

I won't give the whole story away as it's a good movie to watch and quite funny in places, but very interesting when you understand what Spielberg was trying to put across. The scene and statement I loved the most and has stayed with me all my life and is as follows;

Tom Hanks was on his way to this remote tropical island with the rich man's daughter (Meg Ryan) on her beautiful sailing yacht... They were sitting on the deck one evening in the moonlight and watching the stars and the calm ocean when Tom Hanks says something like,

"Wow, This is all so unbelievable, how you live your life, the yacht, travel and everything..."

She then says,

"My father says that almost the whole world is asleep... Everybody you know... Everybody you see... Everybody you talk to... He says that only a few people are awake and they live in a state of constant total amazement...

CHAPTER 2

How do we define freedom?

C an you lock your door tomorrow morning, take a taxi to the airport and purchase a ticket to Japan or wherever and go live in a hotel or apartment for three months or even a year?

I used to be able to do that when I was newly divorced and in my forties, but I can't now as I've been very happily married to my lovely university educated Thai wife for fifteen years and we own a small hotel resort in Issan, Northeast Thailand. But one of the main reasons I personally chose to live Thailand, was to get out of the highly taxed, politically correct and increasingly controlling United Kingdom. Europe and the UK are basically finished now and at the time of writing, there are thirty six Muslim mayors, the home secretary and mayor of London are Muslim, Halal meat is already in most schools and many supermarkets without the permission of the predominantly Christian population. Immigrants are being let into Europe by the millions and breeding faster than the indigenous populations.

Remember the old saying,

"See Italy before you die"

Well, you had better hurry up because, Italy, Greece, France, Sweden, Denmark, Holland, Belgium and even Switzerland are so different now, it's probably too late.

I took my wife to Paris last year and it was incredibly scary to say the least, graffiti for miles along the route between the airport and Paris Central. Gangs of nefarious looking Moroccans and Algerians hanging around everywhere, Africans touting the tourists, police chasing large groups of thirty and more illegal street sellers through the streets. People begging and living on the streets everywhere. Groups of four armed police or maybe they were the army, patrolling the streets all over Paris...!

It was absolutely horrible compared to my last trip some five years previously.

Another old saying comes to mind,

Import the third world and you become the third world.

Unfortunately, they don't have any intention of integration, they just bring every town, city and country down to their level, like a cancer.

Can Europe ever recover?

I doubt it, because of the numbers, they seem to have been allowed entry to destabilise the west. It looks really bad and the politicians and controlling elites behind the scenes, who have no intention of listening to the people, live in their own little elitist bubbles with no care about how the citizens of their countries have to try to live on a very basic income!

So getting out of the corrupt system is probably a good idea in these very unstable times. We will talk more about that later.

So how was I able to travel and live freely before?

When I was in my forty's I was newly married to my first Thai wife and she came with me to whatever country I chose to go live and work in. We lived in Cape Town, South Africa, the Philippines, Indonesia, New Zealand, Australia, USA and of course Thailand. At the time, I was self employed and working as an Independent Distributor for an International Health and Nutrition company. And because they have distribution centres in over fifty countries around the world, one could go live and work in whatever country you choose.

However, there are now so many businesses that can be operated via a laptop anywhere in the world with an internet connection. I've met FOREX traders, website designers, SEO, Wholesalers, Drop shippers, Crypto traders, Consultants, Network marketers, Travel blog writers, YouTube creators, the list goes on and on.

So if your main reason for not being able to jump on a plane and go live wherever you want is YOUR JOB... then you need to change what you do now, to something like the above. I introduced a friend of mine to Thailand some twenty five years ago and he still lives here to this day and now owns several apartments and houses in Thailand and the UK. What does he do? He sells silver jewellery from his website, and Ebay and ships it all over the world.

CHAPTER 3

Things that hold you back

Another big thing that holds people back, is being in a relationship with someone who does not share your passion to be FREE. That's a big one and held me back many times over the years. If your partner is settled in an area with their friends, a job or career, they normally do not want to change their situation.

Obviously, being married, having school aged children, a career that you love and a whole host of other excuses... will also hold you back.

However, IF you are with a partner that does share your vision of being free and travelling or living off grid, then you are incredibly lucky and can escape the bonds of working a job you hate, just to survive and pay your rent and bills. The main thing is, to escape from all the control, taxes, high rents, licences to do almost anything, red tape to start any business and DO WHAT YOU CHOOSE everyday and NOT be a slave to the system.

If you are lucky enough to have enough money in the bank and do not have to work, maybe have investments or whatever, you don't really have a problem. However, even my mate in Thailand has money worries, and I cannot get him to understand how well off he is, and what an incredible free and easy life he lives. He actually owns five houses and apartments, all paid for with no money owed to the bank. Four are rented out through various agencies and he is still worried about his income and paying some tax here and there. I estimate he has around two thousand pounds (US $3000) per month coming in.

Could you live with that and not worry? I know I could.

Did you know that even very rich people get really worried and some even commit suicide, because they have lost their fortunes and are down to their last million!

Typical scenario is, you have a JOB (which usually means you're JUST OVER BROKE) or Married with children. Maybe you have a mortgage or high rent, car payments and credit card bill's or loans and basically, you are trapped in the system.

So how do you change your situation.

Firstly you must change how you think about your current situation. Understand that you have been conditioned and programmed to think like you do, hence the situation you find yourself in.

If you have a house with a mortgage, you can either rent it out to cover the bank payments and go live off grid or somewhere cheaper like Thailand or Costa Rica or... the Philippines, the list goes on.... Or sell it. A house is not yours unless you own it outright, and even then, you have to pay taxes or ground rent, so maybe it would be better to get rid of it. The best thing I ever did was sell my house in the UK, it was only a one bed cluster home that I rented out for 500 pounds per month. So sounds good, 6000 pounds per year, however after agents fees, void periods and maintenance fees, I only ended up with a measly 3000 pounds plus all the headaches from the endless maintenance fees, gas certificates, legionnaires disease certificate, electrical certificates, bills and regulations. Then after you sell it, see how difficult and costly it is to transfer your own money out of the UK.

Just a tip, I eventually found a very cheap and easy way; www. wise.com - Then buy physical gold and untracable crypto currencies like Monero and Pirate Chain.

There are a huge number of individuals and couples that have purchased some land and live off grid, doing their own thing and creating a small homestead. There are even off grid communities in every country, I was interested in one in Panama and another Fiji. I even bought some land in Tonga some fifteen years ago, but because I married a Thai and she preferred our hotel and resort idea here in Thailand, I let it go. It was absolutely idyllic and only cost US$1000 for an acre with the most incredible views, overlooking the other islands and ocean. It was on a roll over 30 year lease with monthly payments of $50. If I was single, I would have gone there and built a house or cabin, it was perfect. And the English estate agent who sold me the land had lived there for 20 years, he even told me it was really easy to get a permanent Visa.

I also still own to this day, 20 acres of waterfront land in Bocas del Toro, Panama. We bought it outright with two friends, also some 15 years ago. The intention was again to build a cabin or several cabins for our own use or set up a holiday resort with bungalows on the water. I still have all the plans if anyone is interested. Another idea was an Eco resort or Off Grid community. I still dream of buying a sailing yacht and having it moored there to use once a year.

However, all (my two partners and I) our circumstances changed over the years and I now live in Thailand, running a little paradise oasis with my wife. (But since writing we've been closed for 18 months due to the Plandemic...!) But we don't need much money to live on out here, and to be honest, having no hotel guests has been lovely and we may not bother to open again. The problem for us living in Thailand, is the distance between Thailand and Panama. It's the other side of the world and involves several flights and approx 20 hours travelling each way, not to mention the cost. As for my other two friends and partners in the Bocas del Toro land, one is also married to a Thai and still living in the UK with two children. He also has a house, apartment and a fruit farm over here in Thailand and plans to come live here in a year or so after his two children are settled in College or University. My other mate is also living in the UK with a partner and their son. He loves the idea of moving to Panama and starting an Eco resort or a camping site but his partner is too busy running her alternative food and vegan type business in the UK. Who knows what the future holds, but he is in the best position to do something with it. I would probably sell my share and maybe they would too, but last time we all spoke, we sort of all agreed that, as it is all paid for and the world is in such a mess, we all agreed to just keep it as a bolt hole in case the world goes completely mad, which in my eyes seems highly likely in the near future.

CHAPTER 4

Debts and expenses

Many people are living off grid in a van, motorhome or narrow-boat on the canals but even canal living is getting restrictive last time I looked into it. Parking at night in a motorhome or living in van is also getting harder and harder. A nice live aboard sailing yacht would me my personal choice, if I was with a partner that shared my passion for the sea and nice big yachts. Unfortunately, she doesn't but we are still very happy and live an incredibly free lifestyle together. In fact, we are off to the Yacht and Boat show in Phuket again in January. I've booked a nice apartment overlooking the marina for a couple of nights and the flights are dirt cheap in Thailand at only £45 ($75) each return.

When we were living in the UK and wanted to go to London for the day, it would cost us £45 EACH in train fares alone! And we only lived 30 miles from London, and if we took the car, it was an even worst nightmare for parking and costs.

Let's talk about credit card debt.

Most people owe thousands on their credit cards. But did you know the whole banking system is based on creating money out of thin air and getting you to agree via contracts to pay back interest and capital. Now I am not advocating you walk away from your debts or obligations, but you do need to look into all the ways you can, if you choose, cancel your credit card and other loan debts. I'm not going to go into details here but you can do your own research on how debt is created and how to get out of it legally. Try a search for "Freeman debt cancellation." Most people again, are not informed and actually believe what the banks and debt collection agencies tell them. Look into it.

Wherever you decide to go, you will need some money to live and survive but the first step is to disentangle yourself from the web of ongoing payments the system seems so good at getting us into like;

Car payments - Sell it and buy a cheaper car.

Cable TV, Sky sports and movies - Cancel it.

Mobile phone contract - Sell or cancel. I changed from £50 - 100 per month ridiculous charges to a £10 a month Giffgaff deal... brilliant.

Any monthly payments you don't really need, cancel them. Just keep the basics like broadband and a no contract mobile.

CHAPTER 5

Why Thailand

W ell, I have been all over the world and I do understand that Thailand is not for everyone, if fact I'm always amused when fellow foreigners get angry and annoyed at the way things work or more like, "don't work" over here. The Thais are definitely a race of people that have their own way of doing things. Those of us from the west could literally go out of our minds if we let it get to us, but we all deal with it in our own ways. I'm not going to go down that road here (talking about how nuts they are, the crazy driving and lack of any sense of keeping their beautiful country clean and not dump rubbish everywhere).

What I need to get across to you is, how easy it is to live here compared to the UK, Europe, USA or any other western country. So long as you keep yourself within the law and don't get into any issues with drugs, gambling or anything illegal, you can more or less live totally free and do anything you want.

For example, If I wanted to start a business selling anything in the UK, firstly, I would need permission and probably a license or premises or an expensive market stall. In fact, you need to make so much money to get your new enterprise off the ground, that you'll probably give up the idea as soon as you find out what's going to be involved with all the ongoing costs. Even buying a Burger-van (another failed business venture) was a nightmare with all the rules and regulations and hygiene certificates, all before you even find a pitch (also virtually impossible) and sell your first hamburger.

In Thailand people just set up their wares and sell on the streets everywhere for free. A market stall pitch on a busy market is 100 baht (£2) Car boot sale in the UK is £8 as a comparison.

When we wanted to build a hotel resort on my wife's land, yes we needed to submit plans and use an engineer to draw them up, but after that we could more or less build whatever we wanted, nobody came out to check anything!

What about taxes? We have to pay approximately £100 ($150) per year as we have three bungalows and a pool.

Compare that to our £140 PER MONTH Council tax! (local property tax in the UK)

Living in Thailand can be cheap or expensive. They have everything here the same as, in fact better that the UK. First class hospitals, amazing shopping centres, more millionaires live per square mile in Bangkok than any other city in the world. Do they know something we don't?

So how did it all come together for us?

Firstly, in Thailand to do anything, you need to be married to a Thai. Yes you could set up a Thai company and have Thai partners, but now you're back in the MATRIX or the system of which you are trying to escape from.

My first three marriages were a disaster and I lost a lot of money and wasted time with the wrong partners. However life is about experiences and looking back, I have no regrets and don't think I would change a thing as I learned so much.

LIFE IS A JOURNEY - Not a destination.

And you have to enjoy the journey.

So the biggest issue with doing anything in any foreign country, is having a loving honest and trustworthy partner. And believe me, they are not easy to find. 95% of all Thais (rich or poor) are programmed from birth to "think" that all foreigners are rich and if you can catch one, they will buy or build you a house, give or send loads of money every month, I have written many stories on this subject so will not go into it here. (Amazon; Lambs to the Slaughter books 1 & 2 by Dave James)

By the way, the freedom lifestyle in Thailand is mainly written for guys as I've never met any foreign women who want to meet and marry a Thai man and come to live here. There may be a few out there, but you only ever see girls travelling through or working as a teacher (which is an easy option to come and live here if you enjoy teaching). For me though, that's a "JOB" and like being back in the matrix. The last thing I want is a JOB that I have to do every day, but for someone that loves teaching, it could be a way out of their current situation.

So assuming you have a loving and trusting partner that will "help you" and not become a living nightmare, this can be a paradise on earth. Most Thai girls I've met over the years have a family home, with land that lot of guys like me choose to live on. They will either do up the existing house or build another more westernised style house on the land. This is by far the cheapest option if you don't mind living in a Thai village or farm away from the big cities.

If you're thinking of buying land in a nice area like Phuket or on the coast, it's very expensive, think $50,000 – 100,000 for a smallish plot and then you need to build the house! Doing that is probably ten or times more expensive than living up country in your wife's family home or land. The problem with living up country is, you still need an income to support yourself. Farming is an option and you could have a family member sell it at a local market.

You as a foreigner cannot work here without a work permit. Again I'm not getting into that as we don't want another job, do we? That's what we're trying to get away from. However, It's extremely cheap to live in Thailand provided you don't have your Air Con running 24/7 because your electric bill will be huge. Food is very cheap and we buy loads of fresh fruit and veg from the local market. In fact I can live on under 10 pounds a day and that includes two or three beers, chocolate, and a meal like chicken and chilli with basil on rice or a Penang curry with rice, both less than 40 Baht (one UK pound) at the 7 Eleven.

For years, my dream was to own a small bungalow resort with a swimming pool, I even remember talking to my daughter about it over 20 years ago and she suggested I call it Zen Resort, as she knew even back then, that once I put my mind to something, it virtually always materialises sooner or later. So I was thinking about early retirement at fifty five years of age and because of my last marriage, which I'll touch on shortly, we did not have any money. I was actually renting a house in the UK at a cost of £1200 per month! The council tax alone was £140 per month. Both of us were working and struggling to pay our monthly living expenses. Credit cards maxed out so the debt was seemingly impossible to eliminate.

My options if I was living alone would have been,

* Buy a boat and liveaboard

* Go live on the land I own in Panama (but would need money to build a cabin and all the other off grid stuff I would need) Then create a campsite or basic cabins for all the tourists who visit Bocas del Toro every year.

* Buy and convert a van to live in (Van-life)

NONE OF THE ABOVE were options for me because my loving and trustworthy partner was Thai and did not want to live in Panama, she hates boats and living in a van was not her idea of an easy life. Thais it seems, always want to retire in their home country. They make their money (or marry a foreigner) and build the house or find a guy with a good pension for support. Again for information on how Thai girls minds work and that that they rarely marry for love, it's always a business decision and the guy is deluded if he thinks she actually loves him, see my other books Lambs to the Slaughter 1 and 2.

The land in Panama, again was not an option as it was too far from Thailand. Contact me via the website if interested in 20 acres of land in Bocas del Toro with an 80 metre water frontage, we are open to offers.

https://panamaland.wordpress.com

CHAPTER 6

The Dream comes true

So how did our little bungalow and pool resort materialise?

* The idea or dream was always in my mind.

* My wife had a large family home on one Rai of land (About half an acre.) But she had a mortgage with the bank owing one million Baht or in GBP£21,500.

TO BUY one Rai of land on a main road is currently 3 to 5 million Baht per Rai where we are in Issan. In Phuket it would probably be 20 million up per Rai.

So before we did anything, the bank loan needed to be cleared. Secondly, anyone investing in Thailand, needs to be able to walk away from it IF their marriage fails. Far safer to keep some of your money or assets in your home country. See my book Lambs to the Slaughter for many horror stories but just be warned, whatever you invest in Thailand will probably have to be in your wife's name, ENOUGH SAID.

So what happened to change our situation around?

I unexpectedly came into some money as a house I'd built during my previous marriage to a Filipino of seven years was sold. I had basically put all my money into building a house with a pool in Cebu, Philippines. Again, it was built and paid for over seven years using credit cards and loans and then we got ripped off by the builder. To cut a long story short, we ended up with a half finished house on the hill overlooking the ocean with no legal paperwork or planning permission from the government. By the grace of God, the Universe or whatever is in control of this realm we live in, must have decided that I had suffered enough.

After three years of desperately trying to find a buyer, someone offered me £80,000 pounds for the house. (Finished with planning permission, it would have been worth £200,000.) BUT, the ex wife didn't want to sell, she thought she could keep it all!!! Another long story but after many heated arguments, she eventually accepted the offer and we both flew in to the Philippines to sign the paperwork.

She ended up with 40K and I had 40K.

Now, NO WAY was I bringing that money back into the UK and a one bed apartment was over £100,000, and at age 55, the last thing I needed was more debt. So I paid off the mortgage on my wife's house in Thailand, then paid a 1/3 deposit of £7000 to a Thai builder to build one bungalow and install a swimming pool.

But the BASTARD WALKED AWAY WITH OUR MONEY, he didn't even turn up on the start day. We took him to court and after a year, got some back (£3500) but after paying a lawyer and flights to attend court, the money was all gone.

SO WE TRIED AGAIN

This time we ordered a fibreglass pool (approx £10,000) and it was installed within a week while we were there and during the next three weeks, we over-saw the build of one bungalow. The £40,000 I'd received was now all gone, so over the next two years, we were travelling back and forth from the UK to Thailand, several times a year and using credit cards to build another two bungalows.

In the UK, I was working like a dog doing home removals, my wife was working full time in a care home, I set up an online website business selling car accessories, we started doing Airport parking in the rear garden and even joined AIRBNB to rent two rooms in our house as we lived near Luton Airport, all to make the extra money we needed to pay off the credit cards.

Fast forward

We moved to Thailand five years ago and EVERY MORNING we sit together over a coffee by the pool and are both still amazed at how it all came together and how beautiful our little resort has become with the highest rated reviews on Agoda and Booking.com. I think it's 9.2 out of 10 on Booking.com.

We are now out of the rat race and do what ever we want every day, we don't make loads of money but we do cover our bills and live more or less for free. And to be perfectly honest, we prefer not to have too many guests because the more guests, the more work involved, cleaning, changing beds, swimming pool maintenance. About a year ago we increased the daily rate from 600 Baht to 1500 Baht per night, mainly to keep all the low level Thais away, of whom, are a complete nightmare! Especially the teenage boys, correction, virtually ALL Thai men under forty. All they do is get drunk and jump in the pool making loads of noise, basically acting like children who see a swimming pool for the very first time. The girls are fine as all they want to do is take hundreds of selfies and pictures in and around the pool and gardens.

We don't allow pool parties or groups of young Thai's anymore, in fact, we're very choosy who we allow in. Definitely no dogs, we allowed it once but they let their dog sleep on the expensive rug and the room stunk for weeks and eventually we had to throw the rug out because even after pressure washing the smell was still there.

When my UK pension eventually kicks in, we may not open the resort at all, or maybe put the price up even higher. Several people have asked us if we make money running a hotel / bungalows in our area? The short answer is no, we could if we lowered the price and had lots of bookings, and don't get me wrong, we've been full with all three bungalows booked many times, but then we can go six weeks without a single guest.

Example: When we started building our little resort five years ago, our USP (unique selling point) was, there were no other hotels in the area with swimming pools. In fact there were only about twenty (Thai style) hotels in total.

Now 5 years later, there are over fifty hotels and four have swimming pools.

Even guests that have stayed with us and run hotels elsewhere in Thailand, have told us, our idea of keeping small is perfect because we don't need any staff and if you have 20+ rooms, your hotel running expenses are killing you.

So why is staying small an advantage?

Because our living expenses (with no guests) electricity, water, car and fuel, telephone, satellite TV, and food is approximately 20,000 Baht per month (£450). With guests the expenses obviously rise, electricity and pool maintenance is the worst, but we only need ONE bungalow rented at 1500 Baht per night to bring in 45,000 Baht per month.

SO at 50% occupancy = 67,500 Baht per month.

Over 100,000 Baht is possible with only three bungalows but because of all the other hotels that have sprung up and our location which is 15 km from the nearest big town, bookings are low AND we are the highest priced hotel in the area.

However, we are more than happy and get to live for free in a beautiful setting with virtually non existent taxes or hassle. Our location is also opposite a huge lake and nature reserve, two minutes from a 7 Eleven, Fresh fish and food market, Post office, Banks, Garages and all kinds of local shops. In fact, we could live in our village without ever venturing into the city. Local people come by every morning selling fresh duck eggs, all kinds of Thai style food, not that I eat that much Thai food, just not my cup of tea as we say in good old Blighty.

I've converted the upstairs part of the old Thai house to a huge modern one bed apartment with it's own western style kitchen, fridge freezer and all electrical appliances, nice lounge and outside have a covered terrace overlooking the lake where I spend most of my time. I'm even writing this from that very spot. The wife has just brought me a couple of cans of Budweiser, a bag of my favourite steamed peanuts and three corn on the cobs from the local market all for only 164 Baht (£3.60). Truly freedom in paradise, for me anyway, you might want something completely different.

How much did it cost to build? £60,000 (including paying off the loan to the bank.) But as we keep improving that figure is now up to about 95K. In the UK, I couldn't even buy I one bed flat in my home town for less that 100K and then I'd be back in the matrix again because one still need to find at least £500 per month for council tax, electricity, gas, transport, food etc. The list is long.

If I had to choose between living aboard a yacht, in a van or live in Thailand like I do now, Thailand wins hands down. Second choice, if anything happened and I had to leave Thailand, I'd be looking at buying a liveaboard sailing yacht and learn how to sail.

IT'S NOT ABOUT MAKING MONEY

IT'S ABOUT DOING WHAT YOU LOVE TO DO EVERYDAY

Yes we all need some money to survive, but escaping from the matrix gives you loads more options and most people living in vans, boats or like me on land in another country, NEVER EVER want to return to the old way of working everyday just to pay the bills..

CHAPTER 7

Typical day in paradise

Most mornings after a coffee with my wife by the pool, I'll spend an hour or so in the garden, cutting hedges and keeping the palm and coconut trees trimmed. Then I take our two rescue dogs for a walk around the lake and on our return, they love to play Frisbee, jumping in the swimming pool and having a swim around. By now it's around 8.00 and I might take the kayak out on the lake with Coco one of our dogs or clean the pool or do a few maintenance jobs.

At 9.00 it's my meditation hour and after that, open my writing App and get into my main passion of writing and editing, this is what I love to do and now have approximately 140 books on Amazon Kindle under different genre's and pen names. I try to upload one or two new books per month which brings in about £500 to £800 pounds per month from 8 countries, not a bad income for doing something I love and only wish I'd found my passion sooner.

Then around lunchtime we'll either pop out to a nice restaurant in town but usually I like to cook as everything is available locally and we even have a Costco a ten minute drive down the road. After midday it's usually too hot to be outside, so back to my writing for a few hours. Occasionally I get stuck in the middle of a story (writers block) so time for a couple of beers, go down for a swim in the pool, lay in the hammock under the coconut trees or sit in the cabana and meditate which clears my mind and brings new ideas for the book I'm working on. Being in such a stunning and beautiful setting relaxes my mind and the story line becomes clear.

In Thailand it gets dark about 6 or 7 o'clock depending on time of year, so it's time to catch up on the REAL news for an hour or so via the many alternative news channels like Brandnewtube, Brighteon, Bitchute, Odysee, Rokfin or Rumble. The censorship on YouTube, Facebook and the Mainstream media is so bad now it's quite frankly pathetic and unwatchable. And if I'm still awake, I'll watch a movie.

And because we are only a 45 minutes drive from Khon Kaen airport, we look out for cheap flights on AirAsia to Phuket, Bangkok, Chiang Mai or Krabi, so every few months we have a three or four day mini holiday.

But to be perfectly honest, everyday is like a holiday for me now.

I hope this short book has inspired you to break out of the crazy control system and change your life to live in freedom. I understand Thailand is not for everyone but the same concept and lifestyle can also be achieved in other countries.

Lastly, I'd really appreciate if you could leave an honest review on Amazon, it really helps me and the book being found in the Amazon searches.

All the best for now,

Dave James

davespersonalmail@gmx.com

My other two books about Thailand are below

Lambs to the Slaughter: Love, Scams and True stories of Thai girls and more

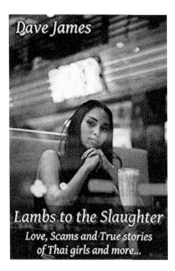

BOOKS BY THIS AUTHOR

Lambs To The Slaughter

A collection of horror stories and weird events. Everything you read in this book are true accounts of actual situations or things I have personally been through and stories about people or events that have happened in the crazy land of smiles – Amazing Thailand.

Lambs To The Slaughter 2

I'm Dave James, currently 65 and been coming to Thailand for 26 years and been married four times. My first wife was white British like myself, of whom we had two daughters, both now grown up and given us six grand children. My next wife was Thai (7 years) and mentioned in my last book, then a Filipino (5 years) briefly mentioned in this book and lastly my current Thai wife of over 11 years. We are incredibly happy and have built a bungalow and pool resort where we currently live in Thailand.

So believe me, I know what I'm talking about when it comes to Thai and Filipino girls and have seen literally hundreds of cases of foreign guys like myself losing everything because of their cunning mentality and scheming nature.

This book covers one of my own nightmare stories, several new stories and a follow up from a couple of stories in my previous book.

Printed in Great Britain
by Amazon

84153311R00020